CAT COLOR
BOOK

James Sasso

About the artist:

James Sasso is an artist, yogi and nature lover. He paints abstractions in color or black and white. He likes to paint large paintings on canvas or mural sized walls, among other things. Sasso has also written and illustrated a series of graphic novel style children's books which deal with outer space and our environment, titled Space Junk, Space Junkers and Space Junks, respectively.

Sasso is also known for drawing a collection of numerous cat characters in cartoonish style form and are original depictions developed in his imagination.The stylish cats are enigmatic and fanciful visionary ideas. These cat paintings and drawings often depict an original universe, complete with architecture,society and a landscape, all populated by his cats.These conceptual cat pieces are an integral component of his oeuvre. Some are inside this book. For more information or to contact him, please go to his web links as follows..,

His personal site is ARTTOGO.com

Instagram - Sasso the cat

facebook - JamesSasso1

Twitter -- Space_junkers

CAT COLOR

A collection of ink drawings and coloring book

ISBN - 13 - 978 - 1519544865

ISBN - 10 - 1519544863

The very consciousness of Life that every man feels within him, comes not from something belonging exclusively to himself as a separate or personal thing. On the contrary, it belongs to his Individuality, not to his Personality, and is a phase of his consciousness or "awareness" of his relationship to the One Universal Life which underlies his existence, and in which he is a center of consciousness. Do you grasp this idea? If not, meditate and concentrate upon it, for it is important.   You must learn to feel the life within you, and to know that it is the Life of the great Ocean of Universal Life upon the bosom of which you are borne as a centre of consciousness and energy. In this thought there is Power, Strength, Calm, Peace and Wisdom. Acquire it, if you are wise. It is indeed a Gift from the Gods. ~ Ghani Yoga
yogi Ramacharaka

Hello
My name is:

CAT
WORLD
POWER

FIGHT
THE
GOOD
FIGHT.

the
Hand
of God.

the history of Cats
was not written with
one word.

from the past
going on.
we are many
we are
one.

It began the way
it began.
From where you is,
from where you am.

Calm

Art evolves

all dressed up and nowhere to glow.

Yeow! Yeow!

Yeow! Yeow!

A.

Art is not reality

sleep

Calm

the
Hand
of God.

Look up

There were many terrible things in my life, but most of them never happened. —Montaigne

Look up

Now and Zen.

Every cat has it's day.

ANGRY
CAT
YOGA
ASANA

CRAZY CAT LADY

CAT COLOR

BOOK

James Sasso